Carolina
Love Letters

Carolina
Love Letters

Karen Stokes

SHOTWELL PUBLISHING
Columbia, So. Carolina

Produced in the REPUBLIC OF SOUTH CAROLINA by

SHOTWELL PUBLISHING LLC
Post Office Box 2592
Columbia, So. Carolina 29202

ShotwellPublishing.com

Cover: "The Lovers Walk." New York : Published by Currier & Ives, [between 1856 and 1907]. Courtesy Library of Congress.

Cover Design: Hazel's Dream – Boo Jackson TCB

ISBN-13: 978-1-947660-03-8
ISBN-10: 1-947660-03-9

10 9 8 7 6 5 4 3 2 1

CONTENTS

Introduction

I N THE CENTURIES BEFORE electronic communication such as telephone and the Internet began to dominate most parts of the world, the primary way that people communicated with each other over distance was through letter writing. Nowadays, this practice is often regarded as dead or dying out, and many fewer people sit down with pen and paper to compose a message to someone else. In earlier times, however, and even through much of the twentieth century, it was a common practice, and those of us alive today are fortunate that so many of these documents survive – documents which open up a very personal window into the past and help us to understand the people and culture of an earlier age.

Much of the Victorian era was an era of romanticism, an artistic and intellectual movement that was especially influential in literature, painting, and music. In America and Europe, this era was a golden age of novels, poetry, and letter writing, and – judging by many of the love letters written during this period – also a golden age of romance, as in romantic love. One of history's great love stories took place in the Victorian period – that of the British queen for whom it is named.

In her personal journal of 1840, young Queen Victoria wrote about the first evening of her married life: "I *never ever* spent such an evening. My *dearest dearest dear* Albert sat on a footstool by my side, and his excessive love and affection gave me feelings of heavenly love and happiness I could never have hoped to have felt before! He clasped me in his arms and we kissed each other again and again! His beauty, his sweetness and gentleness – really how can I ever be thankful enough for such a *husband.*" Later, Queen Victoria would attribute much of her popularity to the example of domestic virtue that she had set for her people by her loving marriage and home. Like any other couple, Albert and Victoria had their differences and challenges as husband and wife, but their love for each other proved to be a deep and abiding one.

In the nineteenth century, and especially during the Victorian period, women were admired for their grace and physical attributes, but it was generally accepted that true beauty also required virtue, and the virtues most valued in ladies were those of modesty, piety and chastity, as well as devotion to home and family. These were the characteristics which inspired the ardent devotion and admiration of suitors and husbands.

As far as ideas about love, marriage and the proper sphere of women were concerned, it could be argued that Southerners were the most Victorian of the Victorians. As David D. Wallace wrote in his history of South Carolina, "The unsurpassed virtue of Southern women cannot be disputed." Wallace attributed their virtuousness in part to "the chivalric regard for women fostered by Southern society," and he quoted a nineteenth century visitor to the South, Frederick Law Olmsted, who observed that "the women of the South are unexcelled in the world for every quality which commands admiration, respect and love."

The counterpart of the Southern lady was, naturally, the gentleman, whose conduct was to be guided by duty and honor. In the South, the *beau ideal* of a Christian gentleman was embodied in

Robert E. Lee of Virginia, who, as a general of the Southern army during the War Between the States, was beloved and idolized by his soldiers as much for his goodness and selflessness as his military prowess.

David D. Wallace noted that the morals of the southern gentleman of the antebellum era were generally superior to those of earlier generations:

> Standards of private and public conduct were higher in the generation before 1860 than earlier in South Carolina. The frank grossness of the eighteenth century and the cynical degradation of the Regency disappeared before the invigorating of all the churches following the Wesleyan revival and the toning up of religion and morals by the Evangelical and Oxford Movements, etc., in England and America. Things were done by men of the generation before 1783 that would not be done by men of the same class of the generation before 1860.

Wallace added of the upper class of this later generation, "Its standards of personal and family honor and pure public service, powerfully permeating classes much wider than its own, are the priceless heritage of the old South, sadly neglected by the new."

Of course, many individuals fell short of cultural ideals in various ways, but those ideals were nevertheless aspired to and highly valued among most Southerners. In 1866, Gabriel Manigault, a South Carolina planter and attorney, offered his assessment of the planter class in his state as it existed before the war in his essay "The Low Country of South Carolina," writing: "Among the white population there, as elsewhere throughout the world, too many who had enjoyed the advantages of education, of good society, and the opportunities of moral and religious improvement, were neither well informed, well bred, nor virtuous. Yet nowhere could you more easily find cultivated intellects, pure morals, elevated sentiments, a fervent piety and a strong sense of duty, among either sex."

Though the passions of Southerners were restrained by certain strict conventions and proprieties, social and religious, they could nevertheless express ardent feelings in their letters. Some of the most beautiful love letters ever written come out of the nineteenth century, and many flowed from the pens of the men and women of South Carolina in the antebellum period, as well as during the four tumultuous and heartbreaking years of war from 1861 to 1865, and even in the tragic decade afterward.

The love story of Louis Manigault and Fannie Habersham provides a touching illustration of a love that endured four of the bloodiest and darkest years in American history and part of the turbulent and difficult period in the South that followed. In 1857, Louis Manigault, a member of a wealthy, refined family of Charleston, met the beautiful Fannie Elizabeth Habersham, who came from a prominent family of Savannah, Georgia. Their wedding took place in December of that same year, and the marriage was a happy one until Fannie's untimely death in March 1868 at the age of thirty-two. Unfortunately, few of his love letters to her have survived – Fannie herself requested Louis to destroy them – but his affection and admiration for his wife is evident in a memoir he wrote in which he described her as "the very Perfection of a Wife and Mother, a perfect Christian and an unselfish Woman."

Louis and Fannie struggled through the arduous war years in the 1860s, and afterward, through even more difficult circumstances; as he recalled she was a source of strength and comfort to him in all their trials:

Future Generations will never be fully conversant with the trials we Confederates were made to feel, with the failure of the Cause. In my own case piece by piece I parted with my entire furniture, carpets, silver &c, to save us from starvation. This was a trying period in my life, but in the midst of all our sufferings my noble Wife sustained me; remarking that for her she 'cared not if cast upon some barren Isle, remote from all civilization, as long as we two were only together.' These are moments when the true character of some Women shines forth in all its splendour, & Man feels blessed in having such a support. With a true Christian love existing between Man & Wife, unsullied, and free from Worldly ideas of pecuniary gain, it is astonishing the soothing tendency it bears against trials the most profound. Marriage without affection had best never take place.

In all cultures and classes, there are individuals and families who are more or less religious than others, or not religious at all, but in the South, traditional, Biblical Christianity was a deep and pervading influence in society. Chester F. Dunham wrote: "Southern Christianity, or the theological position of Southern Christian Churches, was thoroughly orthodox. Religion in the South, by and large, supported the civilization, culture, and social order south of the Mason Dixon line." Most of the writers of the letters in this book were devout Christians, and two were clergymen, but they were also human beings subject to all the yearnings and needs of the human heart. Like Adam in the Garden of Eden, these men found that it was not good to be alone, and so they sought for that "other half" created for them by God.

In his later years, William Porcher DuBose, one of the lovers whose letters are included in this book, penned this beautiful reflection on married love: "The human love comes simply because of the fact that the man is made for the woman and the woman for the man, and neither is complete or satisfied without the other."

CHAPTER ONE

DEAREST JEANNIE
THE LETTERS OF R.K. PORTER

A NINETEENTH CENTURY SOUTHERN Presbyterian clergyman might seem an unlikely author of romantic, passionate love letters, but in the 1850s, Rev. Rufus K. Porter of South Carolina wrote dozens to his wife Jane, who was also called Jeannie. The Porter marriage was without doubt a love match, and during the years of their union chronicled in Rev. Porter's letters his devotion to her only seemed to grow stronger and deeper, especially during periods when they were forced to live apart because of his pastoral duties or her health. There were even times when the young minister feared he might love his wife too much. In one undated letter, he thanked her for her last "sweet letter" and confided:

> My own Darling you can have no idea how much good it has done my anxious loving heart. It came like oil on the troubled waters, as cooling water to the thirsty ground. I am afraid sometimes my own sweet one that I love you above my God. I pray not, yet when I think of you in some connections I am trembling lest you are dangerously dear to me. You yourself might well fear if you could look into my heart & see how absolutely and entirely you are entwined

with every thought, every joy, every wish, every hope & desire. How you are enthroned in the deepest & holiest sanctuaries of an anxious bosom and indissolubly associated with all that is bright & beautiful & happy ... But I cannot help loving you so. I try to keep it in subjection, but fear I do not always succeed.

Rufus Kilpatrick Porter, the second son of Rev. Francis H. Porter, was born at Cedar Springs in Spartanburg District in 1827. In 1849 he graduated from the South Carolina College in Columbia and in the same year entered the Columbia Theological Seminary. Not only well-educated, he was also described as having a "highly cultivated mind, enriched by extensive reading" and by "travel in foreign lands." In 1852 Porter was licensed to preach and pastored churches in Waynesboro and Bath, Georgia, where he became known as a compassionate, diligent, faithful pastor.

In 1853 he married Miss Jane Sophia Johnston of Winnsboro, South Carolina. She was the daughter of planter Samuel Johnston (1769-1853) and his third wife Elizabeth Crawford.

On December 6, 1852, Porter wrote the following lines to his future father- and mother-in-law about their daughter:

> To make the future of _her_ life as bright and happy as it has been under a father's roof shall be my study and delight ... You will not suppose me to exaggerate or use merely formal terms when I say I have no _earthly_ hope or joy but what is bound up in her welfare and happiness.

His other letters written during their engagement reveal his anticipation of their upcoming nuptials and his loneliness and longing for his fiancée during a long separation. In one dated

November 19, 1852, he lamented the brevity of her letters to him and tried to explain how important they were to him.

> I am weary of the days until I see you and rejoice that they are so nearly gone. It seems an age since I bade you goodbye. It is so provoking that you wouldn't write to me more. 'Satisfied with a <u>few</u> lines' indeed! I believe I can repeat your last from memory verbatim … I learn more of your character, and more truly understand you from what you have written than perhaps anything else. And every line has only added an additional tie to my heart and bound it still closer and closer to you.

He added this postscript: "I will drop the formal 'Miss' since you did not say anything to the contrary." The remainder of Porter's letters written to his fiancée open with "My dear Jane" (instead of "Miss Jane"), and his first one penned after their marriage, dated July 29, 1853, begins with "My own sweet Jeannie." In August 1853 he wrote to his wife:

> I am possessed day & night with a consuming desire to be with you, to fly to you at once. I know not how it is my Precious, but I feel that I have never loved you as I do now. You were never so dear to my innermost heart, so loved by all the power & energy of my being. And I cannot again give my consent to so long a separation.

Despite the clergyman's objections, however, there were continued separations over the next five years, some due to Mrs. Porter's delicate health. The couple was parted again in the spring of 1855, when Rev. Porter attended the General Assembly of the Presbyterian Church in Nashville, Tennessee. His letter of May 23 expressed his great need for her:

Oh Darling I really do very poorly without you. I have become so dependent on you for so many things, that I cannot get along at all. It is a poor sort of body that has lost its right hand … Take care of yourself, Baby … My home is your heart & arms Darling!

Later that year, writing from Bath, Georgia, Rev. Porter poured out his concerns over his own imperfections to his wife:

I cannot tell you Darling, how painfully anxious I am to fold you once more to my bosom. I feel so imperfect & lonely when you are away. I am often very sad, Dear, when you are here, sad for myself, my own poor erring, sinful nature. Mournful & evil thoughts wh[ich] I could not utter sometimes fill my heart & cast on it the shadow of a great care, and when are from me it is still darker. Love me, bear with me my Darling wife, be patient with my impatience. Fold me in the arms of your tender & forbearing love. Don't let me make you as bad as I am, but strive to make me gentle & loving & tender as you would have me.

In another letter Rev. Porter again mourned his own defects and confessed that he sometimes wished he had a less sensitive, affectionate nature:

Do my own dearest, do … bear with all my infirmities of every kind. Oh be gentle toward my wanderings, and cling to me & love me though I may be so much less than you once dreamed me. Your love is the life of my heart, and it cannot exist without it. I know I should be to you a hundred times more than I ever have been, and the memory of all my defects is often bitter sorrow I assure you. But still my heart cries to you from its most sacred chambers, cries with an earnest & hungry anguish 'Love me! Oh love me still, my

Darling.' I have sometimes sighed & prayed for a less sensible nature, for a colder heart, instead of praying for more control over the one I have. Did I feel less I should suffer less. But wounds of any sort always leave their scars upon me, and I recover from them most slowly. Wrong, very wrong I know, but still no easy matter to lay aside the evil. You must help me Darling, won't you? Would to God our hearts were afresh baptized by His spirit, united wholly in the lofty aim of living only to His honour & glory.

There are a number of undated letters in the Porter correspondence, but from the context they appear to be of the same time period as the others, ranging from about mid-1853 to 1858. They are full of Porter's continued lamentations over the couple's separation and expressions of his yearnings and love for his wife. The following passages taken from two letters written from Augusta, Georgia, are characteristic:

You don't know how I love to gaze over the Carolina side of the river, into that dear old state in which my Darling is. Oh dearest and best of all the earth! How my poor heart is longing for you today! Yet the time is coming on, we soon shall meet and <u>what</u> a meeting my Darling. I sometimes think I should scream for joy, to fold once more my own blessed Jeannie in the arms of fervent and all absorbing love! Oh it will be too much happiness. I feel my eyes filling & my heart leaping at the bare thought. Let me see you once more and I shall be perfectly happy. I am anxious about you every hour …

The time is coming on my sweet, dearest heart and all will be ended, and once more we shall luxuriate in the wondrous pleasure of our own fond ardent faithful love – to have you once more in my arms, again on my knee, folded to your own ones leaping heart, to feel that you are once again <u>mine</u>, nearer me, by my own side! Oh it will be so exquisite, so happy! Darling I must find you well, cheerful, blooming & as bewitching as ever … Darling, I love you till I am afraid of every breeze lest it blow too cool for you, of every sunbeam lest it be too warm, of everything lest it should lessen your happiness my own priceless jewel…

During the War Between the States, Rev. Porter took on the duties of an army chaplain, ministering to the troops under the command of General Thomas R.R. Cobb of Georgia, whom he loved and admired. After the war, in early 1867, Porter was called to the pastorate of the Central Presbyterian Church in Atlanta, Georgia, where he ministered for the brief time remaining to him. He died on July 13, 1869, at the age of 43, having suffered many months with a severe illness. His widow received numerous letters of condolence from family members and friends, all of which express a great love and admiration for her husband. Dr. D.L. Buttolph, a fellow Presbyterian minister in Marietta, Georgia, summed up the character of Rev. Porter in this way:

> He was very dear to me. I loved him in the Seminary, deeply, fervently, for his large, gracious, kindly heart. We were much together, & I had the opportunity of knowing him well. I never knew one who had a more sympathizing heart, and whose character was more transparent. He was perfectly free from all littleness & deception, & I have always regarded him as a model of Christian excellence.

Rev. Porter was buried in Oakland Cemetery in Atlanta on July 14, 1869. His beloved wife, who died in 1917 at the age of 89, occupies a grave near his.

CHAPTER TWO

LOVE LETTERS OF
BENJAMIN F. PERRY

IN 1889, DR. HEXT MCCALL PERRY published a selection of his father's correspondence in two volumes. The first part he called *Letters of My Father to My Mother, Beginning With Those Written During Their Engagement*. Dr. Perry's father, Benjamin Franklin Perry (1805-1886), a lawyer from Pendleton District, South Carolina, became prominent in state politics. During the War Between the States Perry served the Confederacy in the capacity of district attorney, and after the war, he briefly served as provisional governor of South Carolina. His son wrote that he was "honored and respected by all who knew him," and that "he loved his wife with a devotion never surpassed and which time only increased … a more devoted husband and father never lived."

Benjamin Franklin Perry's letters to his fiancée begin in November 1836. He was living in Greenville, South Carolina, and writing to his fiancée Miss Elizabeth Frances McCall, who resided in her native city of Charleston.

My Dear Elizabeth,

I returned from Laurens Court, two days sooner than I intended, for the purpose of writing to you, at Edgefield, by your cousin, Major Hayne – expecting that he would leave here on Thursday … Next to seeing you, being with you and catching the soft melody of your words as they fell from those hallowed lips, will be the pleasure of writing and receiving letters from you. This is my only consolation during the six ensuing long, very long weeks.

I have often, my dearest, parted with intimate bosom friends, near and dear relations, but I never felt the deep anguish of a separation until I parted with you on the banks of the Saluda – for I never bid 'farewell' to one whom I loved more fondly, so passionately, and in whose existence were centered all my hopes of pleasure and happiness in this world. That sadness of heart which my last lingering look at you inspired, as you departed from me, still casts a dark gloom over my feelings. Neither the pleasures of society nor the fatigues of business have been able to dissipate my melancholy. But when I recollect the words which you whispered me as we were crossing the river, I feel cheered, and my spirits for the moment seem to revive. Methinks I can almost hear, even now, that low, soft sweet tone in which they were uttered – 'Doubt me not.' 'The proof you require I will give you the next time we meet.' No, my darling, I will not, I cannot 'doubt' you – and oh that 'proof?' How eager I will claim it 'when we meet again.' It ought to have been given when we parted, and that little heart of yours told you it was unkind to refuse. But I forgive you the damages and will claim the proof in December, the debt and interest.

Strange as it may at first appear, Greenville though dreary and lonely, has peculiar charms for me at this time, and I scarcely ever returned to the village with more eagerness than I did the other day. Almost every thing I see in this place reminds me of you; the houses, river, churches, and even streets, have their pleasing associations. It was in the drawing room of the Mansion House [a hotel in Greenville, South Carolina] that I first made your acquaintance – the very spot where you stood is now in my mind's eye. How many pleasant evenings we spent there! It was in that room I first heard your guitar and the still sweeter music of your song. When I see the steeple of our church, rising, as it were, amidst the forest trees, I am reminded that it was in returning from that sacred Temple of the ever-living God that I first told my love. I may almost say that I imbibed from the sermon which I that morning heard, courage enough to make the confession. But no place fills my heart with more delightful emotion than the 'Reedy Falls.' It was on that high cliff, of a lovely moonlight night, that I first felt that I loved you. It was, as you may remember, the evening of my first introduction to you. We stood face to face on the rock, listening to the music of the guitar mingling its soft sounds with the dashing waters beneath. I gazed at your features, and traced in their soft, lovely expression the sweetness and innocence of your soul. I thought to myself that there was never a human face which bore so close a resemblance to an angel from Heaven. From that moment I felt that I loved you, and I determined to humble my proud heart at your feet ...

I have much, very much to write you, but have not room without troubling you with another sheet of paper. Do write to me, my dear Lizzy, the day after you receive this letter. You cannot imagine the impatience and anxiety with which I shall expect an answer. I beseech you by the love you bear me to write immediately.

Give my love to your mother and sisters. I will see you on the twenty-third of December – 'when we meet again,' remember. Farewell, dearest, sweet lovely girl, farewell.

Your sincere lover,

B.F. Perry

Perry wrote two more letters to Lizzy before he received one from her, but alas, her letters to him were not included in the book which their son published.

My Dear Lizzy,

I had the pleasure of receiving your first letter to me the other evening, and I am unable to express the gratification which it afforded me. I have read it over a dozen times, and should you not write me again very shortly, there will be great danger of my wearing it literally out in reading it over … I kissed the seal with fervent lips, when I saw it was a wafer and fondly imagined it had been pressed by yours.

My dear Lizzy, I thank you kindly for the letter. It came in time to soothe my eager anxiety, and I receive it as another assurance of your love. You need not apologize to me for the style of your letters. I shall always read them as a lover and not as a critic, and I hope you will receive mine with the same feeling … Ladies have always excelled in epistolary writing, and 'novice' as you may be, in the 'kind of letter' you so coyly mention, your 'style' and 'penmanship' are above criticism when I alone am to be the judge. However, the letter you sent me had one fault, and that is a very serious one – it was too short. I hope I am not to judge of the extent of your feelings by the length of your letter. If so, and we are both to be judged by the same rule, my love must be thrice as great as yours – yes, three times three, for I write you letters three times as long as yours, and send you three for one!

You seem to think that I have the advantage of you in this 'kind' of letter writing, for you 'can scarcely believe that' I 'have not before written on the subject of love.' Do you, dear Lizzy, think it strange that a heart which has hitherto been callous to love, should have fallen a victim at the shrine of your beauty, your loveliness, and the amiable and bewitching charms and accomplishments of your heart and mind? If you were as conscious of your own power and influence as I am, you would not think so. Never before did I see one in whose manners, person, mind and accomplishments I could find no fault. I had seen others whom I admired for some particular trait in their character, but I always imagined there was some deficiency, some want of that perfection which my heart so fondly and confidently gives to you. I may almost say, my darling, that I am a novice in love as well as in love letters. In my youth, when a boy, I preferred books to company. This preference I cherished, and as I grew up I became almost wedded to my studies and profession. It has taken you and you alone to break this spell…

Anticipating their upcoming reunion in Charleston, Perry wrote to Lizzy on December 18, 1836:

Your kind request that I will see you the same evening I arrive in Charleston cannot be refused by me if it is possible for me to do so. I agree with you in thinking the evening more pleasant and more sociable for a meeting after an absence than the morning … But my dear love, there is one request I have to make – let no one be present but the family. I would destroy very much of the pleasure of the evening's conversation if there should be any company. I shall expect to see no one but you, your mother, Miss Susan and Miss Anne. And if it be possible I will see you the same evening of my arrival. I will not disappoint you. The request you make gives me great pleasure. You cannot imagine my anxiety and impatience to see you and be with you as the time approaches.

After a visit to Charleston during the Christmas season, Perry reluctantly parted from his Lizzy and set out for Greenville, stopping over in Columbia on the way, where he wrote to her on January 4, 1837:

I arrived here this morning about eight o'clock after a most unpleasant and uncomfortable ride ... I have scarcely enjoyed four hours sleep since I left you, and this morning have been busily engaged ever since I arrived. You must, therefore, make all proper allowances for this confused and hurried letter.

I have found a much greater crowd in Columbia than when I left for Charleston. But oh the change from gentlemen to black legs, jockeys and cut-throats. I do not think I ever witnessed a more villainous, dissipated looking set of men in my life than I now find at this hotel. It is race week and the gamblers from every part of the world seem to be in attendance. At this hour, twelve o'clock, they have all gone to the race course, and the house is quiet ...

I find that all my friends and acquaintances here were disposed to congratulate me, or make some sly allusion to my wedding. I suppose they will now take it for granted that I have received a touch of the prunella, as I have returned from town without being married. How these things can spread so far and wide is to me passing strange. But I find that rumor is always in advance of truth. When I get to Greenville, if the news strengthens as rapidly as it has commenced, I may almost expect to see my marriage announced in the papers. But never mind, we will make true in April what is now nothing more than busy rumor.

I shall leave here in the morning for Greenville, having arranged all my business satisfactorily, and shall expect to receive a letter from you on next Tuesday night ... I wish you to write me all the news of the city, and everything which may occur to you relative to my return in April ... I will write to you every week and shall expect you to do the same. And every evening will remind me of those delightful evenings I passed in your society. The remembrance of them will dwell with me ever, to cheer and encourage me in life. By-the-by, the kisses you gave me on parting I have been eating ever since, but they are not as sweet as some you can give.

Farewell, remember me, love me and wear the ring I gave you constantly ...

The following week, he wrote to Lizzy to assure her that she would be pleased with her future home in Greenville:

Greenville is rapidly improving – there are new houses being erected here constantly – new stores opening – and general prosperity seems to environ it ... I do assure you it has, for several years past, been my firm conviction that the upper country would ultimately contain almost all the wealth and respectability of the lower country during the Summer and Autumn. Let the great Western Railroad be finished to the mountains and who will stay in the lower country during the Summer, exhausted with heat, annoyed by mosquitoes, and the victims of fever, cholera, etc., when they can so easily fly to a healthy region and breathe the fresh invigorating mountain atmosphere, drink good water and have cool nights. Then there is something so grand, picturesque and beautiful in the lofty range of mountains which at all times strike the views of the citizen from his house, garden and farm ...

Later, on January 21, Perry wrote to her from Greenville, replying to a letter in which she mentioned his love for books and country life:

> You seem almost to fear my books as your 'rival.' No, Lizzy, neither in the devotion of my time, nor in the idolatry of my heart, need you ever fear a 'rival.' Though I am surrounded by my books and derive from them pleasure unalloyed, yet my thoughts are constantly with you. To prefer my situation now, pleasant and agreeable as it may be, to the evenings I spent in your drawing room, would be treason to my love. Those evenings were the happiest of my life, and I never can think of them without deep throbbings of my heart and a sigh that they are past. It was then that the fidelity of our love was first sealed with a kiss. But oh, Lizzy, when I think of those evenings and reflect how long it will be before we meet again, I am almost phrensied with the thought. Never can three months, and it will be just three months and one day from this night until we meet, pass away more slowly. To me it will seem an age.
>
> You say that you love Charleston with all of its faults, that you admire the Charleston ladies, and ask me if I do not. Yes, my dear Lizzy, I must feel some admiration for the Charleston ladies whilst you are one of the number. And if I had no other cause for loving the city, the fact of its being your home and birthplace would be sufficient to inspire my heart with that feeling. But Charleston has always been dear to me. The generous hospitality and noble bearing of its citizens, their refinement, intellectual worth and literary taste, have always excited my admiration. But above all,

their Revolutionary devotion to their country. I agree with you in thinking that a city improves the manner and tastes of ladies. And you might have added the manners of gentlemen also. But after admitting all this, I must be allowed to express a decided partiality for the country. It is in the country that we are more likely to meet with simplicity, sincerity, virtue, morality, patriotism and religion. There is in the country a freer thought and a bolder grasp of intellect than are usually met in the city. It is a remarkable fact that very few great men in this or in any other country have been born in a large city ...

In February, as the date of their April wedding drew nearer, Perry's thoughts naturally turned to love and marriage. He wrote to Lizzy:

Ladies may say what they please about not loving till the gentleman has told his love and they have had the time to consider it. I never have believed it. It is inconsistent with our nature. No lady can be so blind as not to see when she is loved, and she quickly knows whether it is reciprocal; every impulse of her heart tells her, whether she inquires or not ...

I have argued this question on the principle that a lady should be governed solely by her love. There may, however, be exceptions. No lady should ever think, for an instant, of marrying a man without she loves. No lady can do so. Never shall I forget the indignant scowl of Judge Huger to a lady in my presence some years since, who urged that there might be instances where it would be proper for a match to be found on convenience without love! 'Tell me,' said he, 'that a virtuous woman can marry a man she don't love!' 'No, never.'

In the same letter he added:

Oh! Lizzy, the idea of your living in Greenville fills my mind with a thousand delightful associations. You will then be mine – united with me in love and by marriage as one person, living only for each other's happiness. How delightful! how exquisite the anticipation! But it causes a deep sigh when I think that two months and a half have yet to roll round before these anticipations are to be realized. But you have so willed it and I must submit …

The month of April finally arrived, and a few weeks later Perry recorded in his journal: "The 27th of April, I was married to Miss Elizabeth Frances McCall." His journal continued:

The ceremony was performed at her home, by Rev. Mr. Speer … The second day after, we left on the train for Aiken, and from there in Judge Earle's carriage to Greenville. On our arrival, a great many persons called to see us, and we were honored with a ball. We occupy pleasant rooms at the Mansion House, where we will remain until our own house is finished. When not in my office, I am with her …

I have not been so far disappointed in my anticipation of the pleasure and happiness of a married life. It is the natural state of man if I might be allowed to use such an expression. The greater part of the world enter into it, and therefore it must be the most agreeable. As yet I have experienced none of the cares and disappointments of a wedded life. Judging from what I know and see, I confidently anticipate a life of domestic happiness.

The following is now a candid description of my wife; it is not written with the blind zeal of a lover, but in the candor and frankness of my nature. She is now eighteen years old, of the ordinary height, and weighs about one hundred pounds; her person is slender and well-proportioned, her figure good. She has light auburn hair, blue eyes, fair and most beautiful complexion, the bloom of perfect health always to be seen on her cheeks. Her features are of the Grecian cast, small and delicate, her forehead high and well turned, the nose, mouth and chin as beautiful as can well be imagined. There is a slight defect in the appearance of the upper eyelid and brow, except when in conversation, which gives that part of her face rather a pensive look. The contour of her face is lovely, and she would be regarded beautiful in any assemblage of belles. In her disposition she has softness and perfect amiability. There is no danger of unhappiness from that source. Her nature is kind and affectionate …

Since our marriage we have been constantly engaged in reading. It is my wish to continue it. I wish to read to her all the books which I read myself. And by this means we will improve together. I am now engaged in reading to her. At present we have more leisure than it is probable we shall have in after life. When we go to housekeeping, there will come the cares of a house, next a family of children, and then farewell to leisure time, or time for reading or improvement.

The marriage of Benjamin and Lizzy Perry was a happy one that produced eight children. The house he built for her near Greenville he called "Sans Souci," which means "without worry." Benjamin Franklin Perry passed away in December 1886 and was buried in the churchyard of Christ Episcopal Church in Greenville. Lizzy survived him only by a few years, dying in 1891. The epitaph on her gravestone is a quotation from a poem by James Russell Lowell: "Earth's noblest thing, a woman perfected."

CHAPTER THREE

THE LOVE STORY OF WILLIAM AND NANNIE DUBOSE

WILLIAM PORCHER DUBOSE (1836-1918) was a devout, brilliant young man from Winnsboro, South Carolina, who could safely be described as a saintly genius. A pretty young lady named Julia McCord was apparently the first serious romance in his life. He had just graduated from The Citadel in Charleston when he met a young woman at Ophir Plantation in 1855, a friend of one of his sisters. "She was charming," he recalled, and after spending some time together, William and the young lady grew fond of each other and reached a "tacit understanding." Unfortunately, his father disapproved of any thought of marriage for him at the time, and, after the unhappy young man reluctantly acquiesced to parental wishes, their relationship ended. William later recorded that the young lady "finally married an Englishman who came over and fought in the Confederacy and who became quite eminent in a scientific way." This Englishman was Captain Henry Wemyss Feilden, who returned to England after the war with his wife to become a noted naturalist and explorer.

In 1860, just before the War Between the States began, William was studying to enter the Episcopal priesthood at a seminary in Camden, and was also madly in love with a young woman he had met while traveling in North Carolina, Anne Barnwell Peronneau. Called Nannie, she was from a well-to-do Charleston family and, like William Porcher DuBose, very religious and intelligent.

In the summer of 1860, suffering from a lingering cough, William made an extended trip into the mountains of western North Carolina for his health. At an inn some forty miles southwest of Asheville, near a place called Dunn's Rock, he first set eyes on Nannie Peronneau, who seemed to have an immediate, almost miraculous effect on both his heart and his health. Later in life, in his *Reminiscences*, William described his initial encounter with his future wife while he was seated across from her at the inn's dinner table: "At that table, literally at the first sight of Nannie Peronneau my fate seemed to be determined."

Later that year, William visited Nannie at her home on Tradd Street in Charleston, and by the summer of 1861 they were engaged to be married. He returned to his seminary studies in Camden, but he kept up a regularly correspondence with his fiancee, beginning with a letter written on October 8, 1861:

> I have delayed writing to you a whole long day – no easy matter, I assure you – until I could have leisure & quiet to turn my whole mind & heart toward you, My own dear Miss Nannie. We have just closed our first weekly prayer-meeting, during which our hearts have been drawn, I trust, close to our Savior & close to each other. And now I feel like communing with you, nearer & dearer to me than anything else, except Him who in His great mercy gave you to me.

I am once more established in my dear little room, surrounded by many old familiar things – engravings, books &c. A year ago as I sat thus, I used often to say to myself 'What could God do for me than He has done? He has given me health, friends, pure and moderate tastes & the means of satisfying them, the highest & holiest of callings & an ardent love for it.' But His infinite love has discovered another blessing to bestow upon me. Oh, may it humble me to reflect upon His goodness & my own great unworthiness!

I feel that God blesses me in my love for you, that He graciously uses it as a means of drawing me nearer to Himself …

The fact is, I believe, that my love for you has expanded & deepened my whole nature, that my capacity for loving others has been increased too. I shall be disappointed in myself if I am not hereafter a better son, brother & friend than I have ever been before. That which I believed God was going to effect by chastening, He chose to accomplish by blessing, viz: give me a deeper & more real & practical sympathy with human nature, its joys & its sorrows. I never doubt that He has given us to each other for our good & for His glory …

I have not opened a book yet – as soon as I get regularly into traces I will tell you all about my duties & studies.

There is a mockingbird singing most enthusiastically just out of my window. It carries me back to Tradd St. & into your presence –

'Oh for the touch of an absent hand!'

You must excuse this letter – it is not written under as favorable circumstances as I hope to write hereafter … I hope to hear from you before the close of the week. God guard & guide you!

Yrs most truly & affectionately

W.P. DuBose

Most of the William Porcher DuBose correspondence consists of his letters to Nannie, but a few of her letters to him survived, and her first one, written from Charleston, bears a date of October 11, 1861:

At last a quiet moment has arrived in which I can reply to your most welcome letter, My Dearest Friend. All day has been employed in business which would not leave me calm enough to write until it was duly accomplished, and now I fear I am too late for tomorrow's mail. My morning was spent in answering some of the kind loving letters I have received from your home. Your father's I answered first, taking a long time to do it, for I wanted very much to please him, and did my very best …

Your letter only reached me last night and as I had been longing for it ever since you left, you may be sure it was most thankfully received and enjoyed. These quiet peaceful hours at the end of the day are so well suited for writing that I fear both of us will be ensnared into staying up later than is good for us. We must try to be conscientious however. I am glad you wrote to me after the prayer meeting for your thoughts were still hallowed by their recent communion with heavenly things, and they have breathed some of their own spirit into my heart. In so very active a life as mine there is great need for an influence which will draw one away from earthly to higher thoughts, and which will lead me to carry all my joys as well as trials to my Savior to sanctify and bless them to me. You will I hope always be that blessed influence to me. You see I am depending on you already for a great deal.

We have all missed you very much indeed … I have your likeness open before me now, looking straight into my eyes, but with a much sterner expression than I'm accustomed to see in them. I have not quite forgotten yet how you look with your lips apart ...

I hope that mockingbird sings often for you. Are you quite well?

William promptly replied to her letter:

I don't know which gratified me most, that the people of home should have written to you so promptly, cordially, & affectionately, or that you should have taken so much pleasure in answering them all for yourself. I know that you will have no difficulty in learning to love them very much – and they certainly will not find it hard to love you, if they are anything like me. Sister and some of the others have been for some time distressed by the fear that I was incurably infected with old bachelor tastes & predilections (hateful heresy) & I have no doubt are truly grateful to you for rescuing me from the saddest of fates. I must confess that my views on that subject have undergone some change lately ...

I have just been reading Colossians II, the whole epistle is beautiful. It is sweet to me, dearest, to believe that you love me, to hear you say that my presence or my letters make you happy. But it is sweeter to me to think of you looking beyond me, up to Christ your master & mine, and rejoicing in Him. 'I choose her who first has first chosen Christ' says B[ishop] Beverly I believe. I think I can say so; I pray God to make us both His, really & entirely, lent to each other here 'for this world's work' & for our mutual comfort, but not resting in each other; rather resting together in Him. I will remember you particularly on Sundays, & use that prayer with you from Ephesians. I love to think that there is no limit to the 'closeness' to our Savior which we may attain, if we only make proper use of God's grace. The holiest saint that ever lived was not so holy but that he might have been a hundred times more so. Let us have a high standard, even Christ himself, & when we are nearest to Him, let us always remember to pray to Him to bring us a thousand times nearer.

You see I write very freely & unreservedly to you. Excuse me when I am too much so, but I feel that in writing to you, I am but communing with my own heart …

Still in the midst of his seminary studies in Camden, William wrote to Nannie later in October:

This is the first regular Fall day we have had, quite a relief after the gloominess of the past few days. I hope you are feeling as well & are enjoying it as much as I am. I think one way of worshipping God is to feel and enjoy Him in Nature. We ought to cultivate in ourselves a delicate susceptibility to all the sources of pleasure which He has bountifully spread around us, just as we seek to cultivate in our souls a tender sensitiveness to all sweet & holy spiritual influences. There is nothing that so awakens in me the 'religious faculty' as music, next to that scenery, particularly among the mountains, with waterfalls for music. There is danger in indulging too much in this poetical sort of religion – it is apt to make piety more reflective than practical, more dreamy than real; but I don't think it should be altogether discarded because it may be abused. The deep solemn notes of an organ, being alone during a thunder storm, or on a mountain without a sign of life around me, & nothing but vastness on every side – these things used to, more than they do now, fill me with the most indescribable emotions. It was very delightful to me, but it made me reserved. Since I have been actually engaged in preparing myself for the ministry, I have endeavored by

God's grace to become more practical, to deal more with the awful <u>realities</u> with which we have to do – sin & suffering, salvation, &c. But still sometimes, particularly on a bright, bracing autumn day like this, the old feelings creep over me. I forget for a time what a poor wretched world this is that my imagination is dressing up in such beautiful colours. I see only the <u>beauty</u> of God's creation & think only of his <u>love</u>. And then His numerous blessings rise up before me. My whole frame thrills with a sensation of health, while through every sense come pouring in the rich 'treasures of delight' which He bestows through these channels upon my thankless heart.

And among them all, <u>you</u> come & sit by my side & in your presence, I can think of nothing but truth, & beauty & goodness & love. A Father that loves & blesses us both in His dear Son – a spirit of holiness that draws us nearer to each other in drawing us nearer to our Savior, a providence watching over us, infinite power & wisdom pledged to make 'all things work together for our good' – 'a new Heaven & a new Earth wherein dwelleth righteousness.' Is it wrong to indulge in such reveries – to forget for a while that there is such a thing as sin & sorrow, & imagine this world a Paradise & ourselves sinless & happy? Does not God Himself in viewing His redeemed children, regard them as sinless? Is it not a legitimate source of enjoyment sometimes to look away from ourselves as we are in ourselves & to think of ourselves as we are in Christ Jesus? '<u>Rejoice</u> evermore.' I do not think we rejoice as much as we are directed by St. Paul to do ...

After much soul searching, William left the seminary to enlist in military service for the Confederacy. He became an officer in Holcombe Legion, serving as adjutant to its commander Colonel

Peter Fayssoux Stevens, who was an Episcopal priest. Initially, Holcombe Legion was stationed near Charleston as part of the coastal defenses, and before going to that post William enjoyed a few weeks in Charleston with Nannie. Adjutant DuBose's first letter, written from the Holcombe Legion camp, was dated December 17, 1861:

> I am afraid you are beginning to think my dearest Miss Nannie, that I never think of you in camp at all. On the contrary I am missing you more and more every day. Those sweet weeks in Charleston have spoiled me, and I begin now in reality to long for the time to come when the anxieties & distresses of war all over, we shall no more be separated in this world. As I can see so little of you, I am growing anxious now for a letter; do write as often as you can, & trust me for wishing to write much oftener than I do. From seven in the morning until eight at night & often much later I haven't a moment to spare & at night it is so cold in our tent without fire that our ideas as well as our fingers are stiff. I imagine that if it was warmer & I had a little more time I would take pleasure in giving you as graphic a picture as I could of our Camp life. As it is I know you will make allowances for the difficulties of my situation. I continue to work hard & to thrive in it. I have control of the drill & have been yesterday & today forming an awkward squad, the performances of which, I feel confident, do credit to my judgment & discrimination. It is amusing to see how independent they are of one another, & how firmly each one believes that he could keep step perfectly well if the others did not put him out. We continue to receive applications from companies & there will be no lack of men if we can get arms …
>
> I find it harder than I expected to be regular in my religious duties & to keep up the spirit of devotion in Camp.

It is so different from my former life & my time is so broken up. So much the greater necessity for you to remember me in your prayers …

Good night & believe that you are always in my thoughts & my prayers.

For many months, Holcombe Legion, now part of Evans' Brigade, continued its service in the area of Adams Run, but on July 18, 1862, William wrote "a hurried note" to Nannie to inform her that "we leave for Virginia on Sunday morning." There the Legion would see action at the Second Battle of Manassas, in which William barely escaped with his life. Later, at the Battle of South Mountain in Maryland, he was captured, and then spent time as a prisoner of war at Fort Delaware before being exchanged. Because the unusual circumstances of his capture were not known for a while, his commander and family feared that he might be dead. By this time, Nannie had left besieged Charleston and was living in Anderson, South Carolina, as a refugee. When she learned that William was alive through a telegram in October 1862, she replied:

How sweet it is to write once again to you Dearest. Since last I undertook such a thing, the days have passed slowly enough, each one seeming long and weary with the burden of anxiety and fear it brought. But tonight your telegram has made me so happy that I must send you a little note of welcome home again. Annie enclosed me the joyful tidings that you are safe in Richmond, and I am rejoicing in thankfulness to Him who has heard our prayers and restored you to us. I feel in the first flush of gratitude that I would like to give some tribute to His love and mercy; I trust this will not wear away, but that rather my life may show my acknowledgement of these blessings.

We have all been longing for you very much and yearning to know where and how you were. Think of our actually hoping you might be a prisoner, yet so it was. After the first two days of suspense, I took courage and believed that you must be one, and have ever since felt strongly hopeful.

Not long after his exchange and release in Richmond, Virginia, Adjutant DuBose rejoined Holcombe Legion in North Carolina. Here, at the Battle of Kinston, he was seriously wounded, but after a period of convalescence, he was once again with the Legion near Wilmington, North Carolina. In the spring of 1863, he wrote to Nannie about marriage, inquiring as to whether her mother "might be induced to relent with regard to the duration of our engagement?" Mrs. Peronneau had asked her daughter to wait until the war was over or her fiancé was ordained as a priest. In a letter of March 25, 1863, William wrote to Nannie:

I am sure I am quite grateful for you under any circumstances, Darling, to be perfectly willing to wait patiently any length of time. I submitted very cheerfully before, & am ready to do so again, if you think it best.

But to say that we are to wait until this war is over, or until I am ordained, is to postpone it to a period which may not come for a much longer time than we now anticipate. It is in fact to postpone it indefinitely. I really cannot see that our marriage would make any practical change in your relations to your home & family, as long as I am in the war, & when that is over we would be married anyhow. And whatever be my fate in the future of this war, I cannot express to you with how much more satisfaction I would be prepared to meet it, if we were married. I don't think it would add much to your anxiety & it would add a great deal to my happiness.

In early April, William received Nannie's favorable reply to his inquiry. He responded joyfully on April 9:

> Your letter reached me yesterday, my Darling, and has given me much happiness. It is all that I wanted, and I feel very grateful for it ... Very few had any right to know from me that I have ever made any effort to get married, and still fewer, if any, to know that her objection was the obstacle. However all that makes but little difference now that I have her & your consent. All that remains to complete our arrangements & my happiness now is able to fix definitely the date of my furlough, and that Dearest just at this juncture I cannot do. The demonstration against Charleston seems to be in earnest at last, & the attack has actually begun. We have orders to hold ourselves in readiness to go there if we are needed, & may do so in a day or two ... In this case I apprehend no difficulty in getting off, & in being able to apprise you very soon of my definite plans. Of course I can do nothing while this uncertainty lasts. The great issues at stake in Charleston swallow up in great measure all minor interests, but as I said in my last I am going to act precisely as though the way was all clear, & hope that all obstacles great & small, public & private will be removed, & that the end of the month will see me in Anderson. If I am disappointed in this hope, we will only have to defer it a little longer, which will be the more easily done as the exact time has not yet been definitely fixed.
>
> The prospect of such a step brought so unexpectedly near, seems to have startled & disturbed you anew. You need not fear for me, Darling. I am going advisedly into the 'hornet's nest.' As long as I have your love, I am not afraid of anything else; if love & sympathy on my part can strengthen & comfort you, you need not fear for yourself either. My

happiness is to make you happy, and I long for the time to come when it shall become a holy & sacred duty as well as a labour of love. Oh my Darling, may the God of love bless & sanctify our union to His glory & our mutual help & comfort! It makes no difference what we are in ourselves. He can make His strength perfect in our weakness. All we need is faith & grace, and prayer can bring us these without measure. I am glad that Easter brought so much joy & peace to us both. The prayers & chants & whole service for the occasion was inexpressibly elevating & comforting.

On April 30, 1863, William and Nannie were married in Anderson, South Carolina. They honeymooned in nearby Greenville, and in the summer, Adjutant DuBose traveled to Mississippi with his brigade. From there on June 11, while enduring sweltering weather and many other hardships, the newlywed wrote to his bride:

Besides His direct grace, comfort & strength, God has given me blessings in this world which I am sure would counterbalance a multitude of trials, if I could but always avail myself of them as He designs. The chief of these, my darling wife, & the one of which I do avail myself the oftenest, is yourself.

You wonder whether I realize what I anticipated from our marriage, or whether at this distance it gives me any comfort. I will not undertake to say how it gives me comfort. What has a woman to do with reasons? That it does do so, I am ready to give you all the assurances you need. At least I am quite satisfied now, and I was not so at all before. I feel fixed, settled & better prepared for the exigencies of the future.

In his next letter he mused:

The little marriage episode is over, & you have resumed the thread of domestic life so rudely broken by me a month

& a half ago. Thank you, my own darling wife for the loving memories which you have of me & of the blessed weeks which we spent together. To think that I have conferred happiness upon you, & to be assured that I have still the power of doing so, present or absent, is the source of the sincerest joy to me. May God enable me add, more than I am worthy of doing, to the usefulness and happiness of your life!

Having survived intense combat and many hardships in Mississippi, Adjutant DuBose accompanied his brigade back to South Carolina. Stationed near Charleston in Mount Pleasant, he penned a letter to Nannie anticipating the anniversary of their engagement in 1861:

You may depend upon my remembering the 1st of October, my darling. I do not fear that the day will ever come when I will cease to look back upon it with joy. It would be a sad day for me if it should come. I don't know that I ever went into battle as slowly & with so much trepidation as I did to that house in Tradd Street two years ago. That was the only campaign that I ever conducted & the only battle in which I ever commanded in chief. I thought the campaign proved me a bungler & the battle, a coward, but the true criterion, success, has convinced me that I must have been a great General in both respects. I promise, my dearest wife, that the return of the day shall be celebrated with grateful prayer. This time last year I was in Ft. Delaware. I hope that this time next year I will be at home.

About a week later, William received news that he had been appointed chaplain to General Joseph B. Kershaw's Brigade. In December 1863 he was ordained as a deacon, and in the new year of

1864 began his service as a military minister in Tennessee. In a letter to Nannie of March 4, 1864, he reminisced wistfully about the first time they met at the inn in North Carolina. Nannie had apparently reminded him of the incident in an earlier letter, and he replied:

You speak in a letter which I will acknowledge directly, of my old dinner table glances at Mr. Eubanks'. Although others may have seemed to share them with you, you were responsible for them all. It was never my nature or my habit to be guilty of such ill manners until you tempted me by sitting opposite to me. Then because I was obliged to look at you, I had to look at others too to keep up appearances. I used to feel very rude, but what could I do! It makes me feel desperately in love again to think of those old days. You did not think you had made so deep & wide a breach so early in the engagement. After all however, my Darling, I would not exchange the calm, tranquil, confident love of our sober married life for the feverish, anxious & uncertain excitement of those days, sweet as they were. Still I like to go over them all & recall the incidents & feelings of that eventful period, until I imagine myself dead in love again, trembling with doubt & uncertainty, trying in vain to interpret your looks & to fathom your thoughts. You used to think I had the same looks & manners for all. Do you not know that it is the nature of love to embrace all who are connected with its especial object? I was in love with everybody at Mr. Eubanks' for your sake. You kindled all my devotion even if you did not receive it all. You would not receive it all then, & so I was obliged to give some of it away. You are ready enough to take it all now, and my Darling, I am just as ready to give it. All I want in return is your own. We are well enough paid in each other's love. Let us learn together to become better & purer & more worthy of the love of Him whose love it is much harder to repay, but who overlooks more shortcomings than we can ever discover in each other.

Now in Virginia, William sent a letter to Nannie dated April 30 noting the first anniversary of their wedding, and informing her of the recent marriage of his brother Robert:

I cannot allow this memorable day to pass, my own darling wife, without writing to you, although Saturday is a day on which my thoughts are all required for other duties. I have to preach tonight, besides preparing for tomorrow's work. Is it not strange that after our wedding day was undesignedly fixed the same as Brother's, Robert should have come so nearly being married on the same day. Nothing prevented it but the fact of its being Saturday. You have, no doubt, heard of Robert's sudden determination to get married before leaving for Virginia. The day was fixed for the 27th & I presume it came off on that day. I wish very much I could have been present on the occasion. Robert was in a state of insupportable excitement … I hope he continued to endure it until the momentous evening arrived. In spite of all that was said, I think I was creditably cool & self possessed this time one year ago. Still I am perfectly satisfied never to repent the ordeal. I hope that Robert after one year's experience of married life, will have no more cause to regret his step than your husband has, my Darling. They have in the army a very homely & pertinent (or impertinent?) query which nevertheless involves a generally admitted truth. 'Are you a married man, or a dog?' We laugh very much at Capt. Holmes who lately returned from a sixty days furlough still in the latter category. He claims one great advantage however over his brother 'dogs,' that he is one against his will. Holmes is a very fine fellow;

I have been delighted with him. He is an admirable officer too … I hope he is going to get a good wife. He is certainly very happy in his engagement. You see on this day marrying is the theme which naturally & appropriately suggests itself. The fact is, it is a very popular subject in camp. While I write there is a discussion going on outside of the tent on the subject between a newly married man, an engaged man, & an old bachelor.

As the year 1864 wore on and grew bleaker for the Confederacy, William ministered to the men of his brigade through many battles and hardships in Virginia. One of his most moving letters described a fierce engagement in October in which South Carolinians General James Conner and Colonel William Drayton Rutherford were wounded. General Conner lost a leg, and Colonel Rutherford, his life.

My friend Col. Rutherford was mortally wounded in the centre of the body. We got the General and himself into adjoining rooms in a house where he died yesterday at 1 O.C. p.m. after about twenty hours of torture. I was with him all the time and have never had my heart more wrung by the sight of suffering. He had been trying for some weeks or months to prepare for death, but could not feel that he was accepted & his sins forgiven. As his end drew nearer & nearer he seemed to trust more & more in God's mercy and at the last he told me he was willing to go. But his efforts to be patient under his great suffering were most touching. He felt that it was God's hand laid upon him and never once rebelled. He kept praying 'if it be possible let this cup pass away from me,' and when I asked him if he could finish the prayer he said 'Yes, but not my will but thine be done.'

The whole scene was the most heartrending and affecting that I have ever witnessed. There is another poor young widow added to the number made by this terrible war.

A few days later, William responded to letters from Nannie, one of which had been written on the anniversary of their engagement:

Just after my last letter had been sealed and dispatched, my Darling, on last Friday or Saturday, two of yours were handed me, of the 1st & 6th, the first written on our engagement day. According to the ancient custom that day ought to have been written with chalk but in our separation I believe I prefer ink. May the day never come, my own precious wife, when its annual return will fail to fill me with gratitude and happiness. Your love is one blessing for which I think I have never neglected to be thankful, and the trials to which we have been subjected have only made me value & prize it all the more. It does seem strange to me that our love is only three years old, even dating it from Oct 1861. In fact, I think mine is nearly, if not quite, a year older than that. I cannot speak for yours, nor do I think you can either, exactly. One of these days I will make you tell me approximately when it did begin. I do not mean to submit to having loved a whole year without any return. If you insist upon it, you will have to love harder to make us even. Your 'passing thoughts,' Dearest, are never 'foolish' or idle to me, particularly when they relate to me, and I like your letters best when they sometimes seem emptiest to you. The assurances & expressions of love when they are the most playfully uttered, & seem lightest, are the evidences of what is to me, next to God's love, the highest & most precious reality. I do not know but that this separation so painful and trying has had the effect upon me of elevating & spiritualizing my love, not only for you, but for my sisters

& others. Human affection seems to me a more sacred and holy thing than it used to, and while I believe I have acquired a larger capacity for loving myself, I learn to look with more interest upon the love of others. One thing is true, that the love of God strengthens & sanctifies every other kind of love.

In the spring of 1865, Kershaw's Brigade faced General William T. Sherman's forces at the battles of Averasboro and Bentonville in North Carolina, and finally surrendered at Greensboro, North Carolina, on April 26, 1865. Chaplain DuBose returned home to South Carolina with $1.50 in silver, a horse, two mules, and his servant named William. He arrived in Winnsboro and then traveled to Anderson to escort Nannie back to his family's plantation, Farmington. After the war William ministered to the congregation of St. John's Episcopal Church in Winnsboro, and then served as the rector of Trinity Church in Abbeville. Later, he became a professor at the University of the South in Sewanee, Tennessee. His beloved Nannie passed away in April 1873, but he found solace in the family of faculty and students at Sewanee. He was loved and admired by his students, who urged him to publish his lessons and sermons. He authored several important works in his later years, and gained international recognition as the foremost theologian of the Episcopal Church.

For William Porcher DuBose, his wife's love was "next to God's love, the highest & most precious reality." In one of his books, *Turning Points in My Life,* he wrote about both of these supremely important relationships, and described his extraordinary encounter with God during his youth. This encounter occurred while he was returning from a march as a Citadel cadet:

Three cadets, returning from a long march and series of encampments, and a brief stoppage at their common home, spent on their way back to their garrison a night in a certain city, and returned at midnight hilarious and weary from what was called a 'roaring farce' at the little theatre, to occupy one bed at the crowded hotel. In a moment the others were in bed and asleep. There was no apparent reason why I should not have been so too, or why it should just then have occurred to me that I had not of late been saying my prayers. Perfectly unconscious and unsuspicious of anything unusual, I knelt to go through the form, when of a sudden there swept over me a feeling of the emptiness and unmeaningness of the act and of my whole life and self. I leapt to my feet trembling, and then that happened which I can only describe by saying that light shone about me and a Presence filled the room. At the same time an ineffable joy and peace took possession of me which it is impossible either to express or explain. I continued I know not how long, perfectly conscious of, simply but intensely feeling the Presence, and fearful, by any movement, of breaking the spell. I went to sleep at last praying that it was no passing illusion, but that I should awake to find it an abiding reality. It proved so …

DuBose then likened this spiritual experience to the mystery of the love between a man and a woman:

God has His ways of coming to us, of entering into our world and into our life and making them new: heaven is with us when our eyes are open to see it. There is only one earthly and very far-off analogy which God Himself uses and we may therefore venture modestly to use. There comes to a man the love of a woman, which is different in kind from any other human love. It comes for a reason and with a meaning, for the endless ends of a relation which is the highest and holiest that can exist between mortals, and that is the earthly source and spring of all other human relations and of all human life. What we call 'falling in love' comes to us just as naturally and just as mysteriously and inexplicably as that other only more spiritual experience of which the Lord says: 'The wind bloweth where it listeth, and thou hearest the sound thereof, but canst not tell whence it cometh or whither it goeth: so it every one that is born of the Spirit.' The human love comes simply because of the fact that the man is made for the woman and the woman for the man, and neither is complete or satisfied without the other. The divine love in which God makes Himself one with us comes simply for the same reason, and because of the fact, so perfectly expressed in the ever new old words: 'My God Thou hast made me for Thyself, and my soul will find no rest, until it rest in Thee.'

In another book, *The Reason of Life,* DuBose emphasized the sacred nature and importance of marriage:

The impulse to discredit or destroy institutions that go back beyond all memory or knowledge of man – such, for example, as that of marriage – because of imperfections or failures or abuses, instead of reading their slowly unfolding meaning, and looking forward and patiently working up to their future ideal perfection, however far off, is an impatience incapable of cooperation with Him to whom a thousand years are as one day. The divine intent of marriage … is the highest ideal of human relation and association, of social purity and perfection. Discredit of it, leading inevitably to corruption in it, is poison to the root of human life.

Today, William Porcher DuBose is commemorated annually on August 18 as a "lesser feast" of *The Episcopal Calendar of the Church Year.*

CHAPTER FOUR

THE WAR BRIDE
DECCA SINGLETON AND ALECK HASKELL

THOUGH NOT PRINCIPALLY TOLD through letters between the two lovers, the story of Alexander C. Haskell and Rebecca Singleton is so lovely and touching, it cannot be omitted from other South Carolina romances of this period.

Sophia and Charles Thomson Haskell of Abbeville District, South Carolina, were the parents of a large family that included seven sons who served in the Confederate Army. The grandfather of Charles Thomson Haskell was Colonel William Thomson, a hero of the Revolution in South Carolina. He was one of the officers in command of Patriot forces who repulsed British forces at Breach Inlet near Charleston in 1776.

William Porcher DuBose, a South Carolinian who served in the Confederate Army as an officer and a chaplain, admired the Haskell family and considered his friendship with them one of the great privileges of his life. He especially admired Mrs. Haskell, a person of deep faith. DuBose regarded her as a great woman, describing her as the "worthy daughter" of her distinguished father, and a cultured and accomplished woman who "trained up, in all that adds nobility to noble natures, eight sons, of whom seven served with distinguished gallantry, and two consecrated with their life-blood the cause which they believed to be that of justice, patriotism, and honor."

One of those sons was Alexander Cheves Haskell, who would later become colonel of the 7th South Carolina Cavalry, and his "Lady Love," as his mother described her, was Rebecca Coles Singleton, who was called Decca. Aleck Haskell had met her in Columbia, South Carolina, and spent several years trying to win her affections. Haskell's biographer described Decca Singleton as "a great belle in Columbia and Charlottesville ... Decca was gay, vivacious, charming in society and sweet in her family relations. She was a little thing, with reddish-gold hair, and an exquisite figure, a beautiful dancer and horseback rider. During the last two years of her life she became deeply religious in a very happy sort of way, full of confidence and trust." She was so popular that Aleck Haskell doubted he could ever win her heart, but after the war began, he was sent to Virginia with his regiment, and in a letter from Richmond written in early July 1861, he proudly wrote to his mother and father in Abbeville to announce his engagement to Miss Decca Singleton. His letter read in part:

> I am engaged to be married and intend, if I get through the wars, to bring you as noble a daughter as your hearts can desire. Decca Singleton has rewarded my three years of faithful affection, and has promised to be my wife ... Do try to be as happy as I am, for there are few women so pure, so honest, truthful and noble. I am indeed happy to have won such a prize.

In his book *Belles, Beaux and Brains of the Sixties,* Thomas Cooper De Leon recounted Aleck and Decca's engagement and wedding during the war in Virginia:

> His first marriage was one of the most touching romances of the war. Miss Rebecca Singleton was a dainty and lovely, but high-spirited, daughter of that famed old name. In the still hopeful June of 1861 Mrs. Singleton and her daughter were at the hospital in Charlottesville, crowded so that Mrs. Chesnut (as her diary tells) took the young girl for her roommate. 'She was the worst in love girl I ever saw,' that free chronicler records. Miss Singleton and Captain Haskell were engaged, and he wrote urgently for her consent to marry him at once. All was so uncertain in war, and he wished to have her all his own while he lived. He got leave, came up to the hospital, and the wedding took place amid bright anticipations and showers of April tears. There was no single vacant space in the house, so Mrs. Chesnut gave up her room to the bridal pair. Duty called; the groom hurried back to it the day after the wedding.

The following summer, in June, Decca was about to give birth to her first child. Anticipating this happy event, the famous diarist Mary Boykin Chesnut, who was volunteering as a nurse at a military hospital in Charlottesville, reminisced about the Haskell wedding in her journal:

> June 13th. – Decca's wedding. It took place last year. We were all lying on the bed or sofas taking it cooly as to undress. Mrs. Singleton had the floor. They were engaged before they went up to Charlottesville: Alexander was on [General] Gregg's staff, and Gregg was not hard on him; Decca was the worst in love girl she ever saw. Letters came while we were at the hospital, from Alex, urging her to let

him marry her at once. In war times human events, life especially, are very uncertain.

For several days consecutively she cried without ceasing, and then she consented. The rooms at the hospital were all crowded. Decca and I slept together in the same room. It was arranged by letter that the marriage should take place; a luncheon at her grandfather Minor's, and then she was to depart with Alex for a few days at Richmond. That was to be their brief slice of honeymoon.

The day came. The wedding-breakfast was ready, so was the bride in all her bridal array; but no Alex, no bridegroom. Alas! such is the uncertainty of a soldier's life. The bride said nothing, but she wept like a water nymph. At dinner she plucked up heart, and at my earnest request was about to join us. And then the cry, 'The bridegroom cometh.' He brought his best man and other friends. We had a jolly dinner. 'Circumstances over which he had no control' had kept him away.

His father sat next to Decca and talked to her all the time as if she had been already married. It was a piece of absent-mindedness on his part, pure and simple, but it was very trying, and the girl had had much to stand that morning, you can well understand. Immediately after dinner the belated bridegroom proposed a walk; so they went for a brief stroll up the mountain. Decca, upon her return, said to me, 'Send for Robert Barnwell. I mean to be married today.'

Impossible. No spare room in the house. No getting away from here: the trains all gone. Don't you know this hospital place is crammed to the ceiling? 'Alex says I promised to marry him to-day. It is not his fault: he could not come before.' I shook my head. 'I don't care,' said the positive little thing, 'I promised Alex to marry him to-day and I will. Send for the Rev. Robert Barnwell.' We found Robert after a world of trouble, and the bride, lovely in Swiss muslin, was married.

Then I proposed they should take another walk, and I went to one of my sister nurses and begged her to take me in for the night, as I wished to resign my room to the young couple. At daylight the next day they took the train for Richmond. Such is the small allowance of honeymoon permitted in war time.

Aleck and Decca's days together as husband and wife were to be brief. Thomas Cooper De Leon recorded that within one year after their wedding "the husband was a widower, with only the news from his far-away baby girl to solace the solitude of his tent." Decca gave birth to a daughter named Rebecca on June 20, 1862, and less than a week later, on June 26, the young mother passed away.

On June 27, 1862, Mary Chesnut recorded the following passage in her diary:

Decca is dead. That poor little darling! Immediately after her baby was born, she took it into her head that Alex was killed. He was wounded, but those around had not told her of it. She surprised them by asking, 'Does anyone know how the battle has gone since Alex was killed?' She could not read for a day or two before she died. Her head was bewildered, but she would not let anyone else touch her letters: so she died with several unopened ones in her bosom. Mrs. Singleton, Decca's mother, fainted dead away, but she shed no tears. We went to the house and saw Alex's mother, a daughter of Langdon Cheves. Annie was with us. She said: 'This is the saddest thing for Alex.' 'No,' said his mother, 'death is never the saddest thing. If he were not a good man, that would be a far worse thing.' Annie, in utter amazement, whimpered, 'But Alex is so good already.'

'Yes, [said his mother] seven years ago the death of one of his sisters that he dearly loved made him a Christian. That death in our family was worth a thousand lives.'

The "dearly loved" sister was Mary Elizabeth Haskell, who died in 1855 at the age of 21. In his memoirs, Aleck Haskell described her as having "one of the sweetest dispositions I ever knew. She was loved by all." When Mary fell ill with what was probably tuberculosis, Aleck was her constant companion and "devoted attendant" for six months. The peace and faith she exhibited in her dying hours had a profound religious effect on him and his brothers.

Mrs. Chesnut also recorded Decca's last days and passing in Richmond in her diary. Before Decca died on June 26, about a week after the birth of her daughter, the young Mrs. Haskell told Mrs. Chesnut that she had experienced "perfect happiness" in her married life. Mrs. Chesnut wrote:

> In a pouring rain we went to that poor child's funeral – to Decca's. They buried her in the little white frock she wore when she engaged herself to Alex, and which she again put on for her bridal about a year ago. She lies now in the churchyard, in sight of my window. Is she to be pitied? She said she had had 'months of perfect happiness.' How many people can say that? So many of us live their long, dreary lives and then happiness never comes to meet them at all. It seems so near, and yet it eludes them forever.

In 1934, Aleck Haskell's daughter, Louise Haskell Daly, wrote a biography of him entitled *Alexander Cheves Haskell: The Portrait of a Man.* Only about 125 copies were privately printed, and the author sent one to the famous historian Douglas Southall Freeman, who is best known for his biographies of Robert E. Lee and George Washington. In Freeman's letter of acknowledgment to Mrs. Daly, he praised her father's memoirs highly and asked permission to include one of his letters in a new book he was working on (*The South to Posterity*, published in 1939). Freeman called a letter Alexander Cheves Haskell had written to his mother in 1863 the "one of the most beautiful born of war," and held him up, along with such figures as Robert E. Lee and General Stonewall Jackson, as one of the highest examples of Southern character.

In this beautiful letter written on April 2, 1863, a grieving Haskell opened up his heart and "its agony" to his mother after the death of his beloved wife Decca. He assured her that God had brought him resignation and "submission to His will," but confessed that he was afraid to suffer more loss. "Life and hope are awakening anew and I begin to hug too closely my idols of earth. I dread almost my love for my poor little Baby, lest this too must go."

Alexander Cheves Haskell was wounded four times during the war, most seriously in October 1864, when he was shot in the head. He lost the sight in one eye, but otherwise made a remarkable recovery and returned to his unit in the Army of Northern Virginia to serve to the end of the war. In 1870, he remarried and had more children, but he would never forget his first love. There was "a complete openness and confidence" between Aleck Haskell and his second wife about Decca, and their daughter Louise Haskell Daly ended their story this way:

> As long as our Mother lived she never failed on Easter Sunday to place a wreath on Decca's grave in Old Trinity Church yard. I think she felt, and without any bitterness, that Father never recovered from the wound of Decca's death. It was Mother who told me what I know of the sad story. Father never spoke of it.

CHAPTER FIVE

ETERNAL DEVOTION
FRANK FROST AND REBECCA PRINGLE

T HEIR DEVOTION TO EACH OTHER was deep-seated and eternal," Susan Pringle Frost wrote of her parents. In a memoir entitled *Jottings*, Susan recounted the courtship and marriage of her father and mother, Francis LeJau Frost and Rebecca Brewton Pringle:

On December eleventh, 1866 he married our mother, Rebecca Brewton Pringle. He delighted in telling the story of how he happened to meet our mother. It was in the early part of the Confederate War, when Charleston was being shelled by the enemy by land and sea. While the young men of the families remained to assist in the defense of the city, the women and children were sent, wherever possible, to friends out of town, beyond the reach of the shells, to refugee until the danger was over. Our grand-parents had friends, the Williams, in Society Hill, an old community farther upstate; with her usual cordiality Mrs. Williams took in our grand-parents and our Aunt Susan Pringle and our mother. Our father often told us of how he met our mother, and fell in love with her at first sight, from across the dining table at a family gathering of Mrs. Williams ... He told us of how as he sat opposite to our mother at the dinner table, he fell in love with her, and made a vow to himself that if his life was spared to return from the war, he would come back and marry her. His life was mercifully spared, and he made good his vow, and returned to marry our mother, at St. Michael's Church. He told an amusing anecdote of some of the little nieces and nephews who attended the ceremony. I presume it was the first wedding they had attended, and being well versed in the Old Testament history, they were quite mystified why the wedding united Francis and Rebecca instead of Isaac and Rebecca.

Francis LeJau Frost was born in Charleston in 1837. His education included studies at the Medical College of the State of South Carolina, from which he graduated with distinction in the class of 1861. During the war that began that year, he served as a surgeon on the staff of Confederate General A.P. Hill. Born in 1839, his future wife Rebecca Brewton Pringle was also a native of Charleston. Both she and Frank were from distinguished families, and Rebecca could trace her namesake to a great-grandmother, the Revolutionary patriot and heroine Rebecca Brewton Motte. Rebecca's mother was Mary Motte Alston Pringle (1803-1884), the matriarch of a large, wealthy planter family of Charleston. The subject of Richard N. Cote's book *Mary's World,* she was a devoted mother to her thirteen children, and "inculcated them with the Christian and social values they would need when they assumed their roles in upper-class plantation society."

Like so many other South Carolina families, the Pringles suffered grievous losses during the war that began in 1861. Several of Mary Pringle's sons served in the Confederate Army. In 1863, one of them, Captain Robert Pringle of the 15th Battalion, South Carolina Heavy

Artillery, was killed at Battery Wagner in Charleston Harbor by shelling from a Federal ironclad ship. On August 23, 1863, his brother William A. Pringle wrote to his parents about Robert's death. The following is an excerpt from that letter:

> I was on guard on Southern Wharf on Friday night, when, about ten o'clock, Sam Stoney called me aside, and said he had sad intelligence to give me ... He said that my brother James had been killed on Morris Island ... I left the wharf to make arrangements about receiving his remains the next morning at daylight, when the boats usually returned with the dead and wounded. I had not gone many steps, when I heard someone call my name; I turned; and, to my utter amazement, James met me. For an instant I was really under the impression that I saw his ghost, but as I seized his hand, so little did any thought of Robert's death enter my mind, I concluded, of course, it was all a mistake, till James' single word 'Robert' revealed all the truth. He said he had brought up his remains in a row boat, then at the wharf. We went together to the side of the dock, and there, on a stretcher, wrapped in a blanket, was our dead brother.
>
> We took him from the boat, put him in an ambulance, and carried him into the silent King St. house. There we exposed the ghastly, cruel wounds, and Brewton, James and myself, assisted by the weeping servants, took off his bloody clothes, and laid him in the south parlour.

The war wiped out the most of the wealth and power of the planter class, but life went on, and like other formerly prosperous Southern families, the Pringles and the Frosts were forced to adapt to the realities and difficulties of the post-war period. Frank and Rebecca were married in Charleston on December 11, 1866. As a wedding gift, Rebecca's mother gave her a Bible, and her father presented her with

$75.00, telling her that it was all the patrimony he had to give after losing his fortune in the war. Soon after the wedding, the couple left Charleston and traveled in a buggy to a plantation called Camp Main on the North Santee River in South Carolina. Here, Frank would struggle to make a living as a rice planter for the next ten years, while also managing Richfield, the nearby rice plantation of his father-in-law William Bull Pringle.

About two weeks after the wedding day, Rebecca's mother wrote this beautiful message to her daughter: "My beloved daughter, I have never before understood how disinterested my maternal love is until now, when I find myself rejoicing in your happiness. I love to picture you in your new home, to think of your heart opening to new affections. Of your mind turning to new duties. May the Holy Spirit purify and strengthen you in them all."

Though devoted to Frank, Rebecca did not like living in the country. Her daughter, Mary Pringle Frost, wrote of her early married life: "At one time my mother became lonely and even wept; then my father said there was nothing to be done but take her to her parents. Remembering the well-ordered home and the plantation home in which she, my mother, had lived before the war, it is not surprising that she should at times have been overcome. She came to her parents for the birth of each child."

Mary wrote of her father during these years on the North Santee: "There was a community of planters within a radius of a few miles. Our father was the only physician. He practiced medicine, surgery and dentistry. He did not charge for his services. After working in the field all day, he would go out at night to minister to the sick negroes on the plantations … In the summer the planters moved to South Island on Winyah Bay to avoid malarial fever."

The first few letters from Frank to Rebecca were written in the months just before their marriage. Frank was at Camp Main, and Rebecca was in Charleston with her family. The rest of their letters were penned after their marriage, during periods of separation that were extremely trying for the young husband and wife.

The following is an excerpt from a letter dated October 14, 1866, from Frank to his fiancée Rebecca:

My dear, dear Rebecca,

My absence from you today has been unusually painful. My first thoughts upon waking were of you, and you have been in my mind, almost without interval, ever since. I do long more than I can express to be with you again. My mind <u>will</u> recur to the happy evenings & Sundays, which I have spent with you, in uninterrupted succession, since our engagement. The joys which I then experienced seem only to increase the unhappiness which this separation occasions … My separation from you gives me more distress & uneasiness of mind than I have ever felt from any other cause. My feeling is that I cannot endure it much longer: that either you must live with me, or I with you. We must be together.

This morning after breakfast & prayers I walked round the plantation with my 2 foremen to decide upon work for tomorrow, intending upon my return to devote the rest of the day to writing to you, but, on getting back, I found to my great annoyance a Yankee soldier on the piazza, awaiting me. He came, by my appointment with the P.M. [Provost Marshal] in Georgetown, to arrest a negro on Lucas' place for killing a horse & hog belonging to a man on this place. I did not expect him until this time. Tomorrow he will take the parties to jail.

I expect to begin work in the morning with about 15 hands … They still seem disposed to work & do well so that I am much encouraged, & am quite hopeful of a good result. I find too that there is by no means as much repair & work needed as I had expected, & that the people have made a much better crop than I had supposed, & that they are honest, harvesting & storing it according to the contract. I have no reason to think that they have stolen any of it, & the two foremen assure me that they have not …

I beg that you will think seriously & definitely of getting married, & I hope that you will agree with me in very earnest desire for an early consummation of such a happy event. If we will fully make up our minds to adapt ourselves to our present circumstances & to the exigencies of the times, there is no reason why we cannot live here in contentment & happiness … The single condition of happiness with me is that I be with you …

A couple of days later, Frank wrote to Rebecca:

I cannot sufficiently thank you for yr letters of Saturday & Sunday last. You know I have often told you that you are too good for me, & too good to me; and truly I feel more & more, as yr goodness & character are developed to me, that such is the case.

… I spent the rest of the evening reading & re-reading these cherished lines of yrs; my heart full all the while, even to tears, with the most tender & pleasurable emotions of love & gratitude to you. I would read & then look at yr dear likeness, and be quite overcome with emotion. I need not tell you that I did not write to yr bro[ther]. My heart was too full to admit of any thoughts than of you. And so I went to bed after the most earnest & effectual prayer that I have made in a long time: that God may forgive us & bless us, that He may enable us to live to his Glory, that He may first guide us with His counsel & then receive us to glory for our Savior's sake.

My dear, dear Girl. I cannot tell you what a source of comfort & happiness you are to me. I prize above all things on earth yr tender love & regard for me. I esteem my present relationship to you the greatest blessing of my life. Let us live to love & cherish each other, and to serve & glorify God, with an humble dependence upon his blood, & with a simple, confiding trust in the merits of our Savior. Our destiny here & hereafter must be full of happiness & joy ...

In November 1866, Rebecca's father traveled to the North Santee, and on the tenth of that month, Frank sent another letter to his fiancée:

My very, very dear Rebecca,

Yr good old father has just gone to bed, being much fatigued by the labors of the day. I, too, am tired & look wistfully at my couch; but my mind is always so full of you, that the pleasure of writing to you at once awakens me. I wish that I could send a few lines to you every day to relieve my pent up & impatient feelings; it w'd be so gratifying & pleasant to us both ... If I could only know each day that you are well, it w'd be such a relief to my constant anxiety as to yr health & welfare, wh[ich] distresses me no little.

I hope that the old Gentleman will give a good acc't of things up here, & of his stay with me. I fear tho' that he may not; for I know that I am a very poor housekeeper, & then the house is in such a dismantled state, that there is little comfort to be had in it at present. Every morning when I go to the storeroom to give out things for the day, I think of you so forcibly & think how much better it will be then than now; & how happy we will be together in our own home, with nothing to disturb the free & natural flow of love between us. My hours of respite from business will be so joyful & happy in yr company. My dear Love, yr presence is the only condition necessary to my happiness on this earth, and without the hope of that at some future time, I w'd be truly a miserable man, with no object or end in this life. You are everything to me now. My whole life & being are wrapped up in & identified with yr dear self. Before I knew you & was without you, I had the happiness usually allotted to man; but now I feel that to be without you w'd be the intensity of misery on this earth. Strange! Is it not? but still so.

Well, I sometimes think you must be tired of hearing of my love for you; but, it is the burden of my thought, & so it must be the burden of my song; & this you must consider, & grant me the only pleasure that I have in my absence from you.

I feel so thankful to you for yr letters & am so happy in yr love for me, that these thoughts are always in my mind.

Affairs are going on very well on the plantation. By close attention to business, and … observation of the negroes, I think our prospects of success here next year good. Yr father, like all old gentlemen is at times very despondent, but I, who am more buoyant in spirit & more knowing of free negroes, maintain an even [turn] of hopefulness & spirits. Patience & perseverance are the two qualities required, & I think that I have them by education of last four years. By Jan. I hope to be so advanced in the preparation of my land as to offer great inducements to good negroes to come & contract with me for the year.

Frank's next letter, which mentions his sister Elizabeth, was dated November 12, 1866:

My dear, dear, very dear Rebecca,

Yr letters of Saturday & Sunday by Lizzie, I have read tonight, with how much pleasure, with how much pain & disturbance of mind, I cannot tell you. My dear, dear Love, I do love you with all the ardor & fervor possible; it seems to me, with more than the full strength & capacity of my heart; & yet, I feel that I do not love you enough, & I am dissatisfied with myself on that acct. At times I feel that my only worth is, the love & admiration that I have for you. I have read yr letters over 3 times, the one written on Sunday I read 2ce [twice] while Lizzie was sitting near. She could not help noticing how much I was affected by it ... My sympathy with you is so intimate & perfect that I am greatly affected by anything that affects you. It really distresses me to think that you sh'd be so much disturbed about my old uncle. I am more distressed & disturbed in mind by yr letter tonight than by any other circumstance in a long, long time. As you have lost sleep on the subject; so now will I and, by night & day, I will be brooding on this one subject. If Lizzie was not here, I would go to town immediately to see you ...

My dear, dear Love, it seems that any trouble of this kind only deepens & expands my love for you. I do long & yearn to be with you tonight. So forcible & irrepressible was this feeling after reading yr letters, that I could not help expressing it repeatedly before Lizzie ... Oh! my dear, dear, dear Rebecca, do not let there be any cause of difference between us. The very thought of it brings tears freely to my eyes ...

I do love you with all the intensity, & ardor & freshness of which a virgin heart is capable. The sweet assurances of love, confidence & sympathy in yr letters do fill me with happiness ... more than I can express ...

Frank and Rebecca were married the following month, in December 1866. The new bride was soon expecting a child, and by late summer she had returned to Charleston to await the delivery of her baby. This is an excerpt from one of the first letters written to her by Frank, dated August 13, 1867, during their "first separation":

My dear, sweet wife,

How deeply I feel this our first separation it is impossible for me to say. I have been thinking of you every moment since we separated last night. It seems to me that I love you with ten fold more ardor & purity than I ever did. My dear wife, you cannot think how I miss you; how I long for you; how I yearn for you; how I roam about the house like a restless spirit, my heart full to tears as each object reminds me of my dear, sweet one now absent from me. The thought of you, of yr goodness & gentleness & purity makes me cry like a child. I feel completely heart-broken & desolate without you. You are the only one on earth to me now. Without you life is blank, cheerless, hopeless. But I must indulge longer in this strain; for it only increases in us both pangs of the deepest pain at our separation …

Three days later, Frank wrote to his wife in Charleston from South Island:

My dear, good wife,

I am so tired tonight that I will have time to write only a few lines … I do not do anything with the same interest or find the same pleasure in anything that I did when you were here. I do not care to gather the vegetables or melons, or to put them in the buggy, for I feel there is no one here to take any pleasure in them & to give me pleasure in receiving them … I feel so lonely at night, my dearest one, & I know that you suffer in the same way & this increases my distress.

I long to be with you again. I miss you at every turn & every moment of the 24 hours … you may expect me to have me with you on Saturday night. The thought of meeting you again, my only one on earth, fills me with the deepest & purest pleasure. Without you I have the most painful feeling of being alone & desolate, without anyone to care for or love me & without anyone for me to care for or love …

Evidently concerned for Rebecca's health, Frank cautioned her to take care of herself in a letter of September 29, 1867:

… Yr life sh'd be as quiet as possible now, & free from every possible cause of excitement or accident. I often think of the dangers to wch. you are liable now, & in that connection, or yr habit of running downstairs in such a headlong manner. Do, my dear wife, desist from this. Walk down quietly as other people do. I do long to be with you, my dearest one. The more I think of you, the more I am full of painful apprehensions for yr safety; the more I love & long to be with you. If I was only a good Christian, I could with so much confidence & comfort put you in the hands of God, & thus find a most soothing balm for my painful & distressing fears on yr acc't …

I cling to you with my whole heart and strength, my own good & loving one; for I feel as I have often told you that you are my only comfort, my only joy on earth; without you, the angel, the idol of my heart, I w'd be of all men most wretched. I do so long & yearn to be with you at times, my sweet, good wife, that I think I cannot bear this separation any longer, that I must go to you & then the sense of duty takes possession of me & brings my mind to its proper balance … so perverse is my nature … so indisposed to anything Godly, that I feel myself an outcast & without God in the world; & this tho't in my moments of reflection fills me with fear & misery. At such times I catch the spirit of the hymn, 'Oh! for a closer walk with God' &c. & pray earnestly that God will fill me with the spirit of faith & of repentance, with a loathing of sin & of my own wretched self, & with hunger & thirst after his righteousness & the glories of His kingdom. My dearest wife I can't tell you how unhappy sin makes me & how I do long to be an humbly faithful servant of our blessed saviour & yet with all this, it seems that I grow worse every day, more estranged from God & more hopelessly the servant of sin. Pray for me, my good wife, for I do pray for you with all the strength & fervor of wch my cold, sinful nature is capable.

I lean on you & your ready acquiescence in God's blessed will ... but poor wretched, sinful creature that I am, I have no such faith, no such humble resignation to God's will; so I am the subject of all the miseries & pains of sin. I feel that the case of the Devil is mine, I believe and tremble. Instead of my faith filling me with comfort & joy unspeakable & with the love of God & my neighbor, it fills me with fear & with awful foreboding of death & of judgment & of retribution. I know that God is ... merciful, that he is longsuffering & forbearing in His love & goodness to us, & that He is willing & able to save to the uttermost all who come to him thro' Christ ...

In a letter of November 21, 1867, Frank wrote from Camp Main again, mentioning a visit by Rebecca's father, William Bull Pringle:

Yr father arrived yesterday earlier than was expected & so he had to take a seat up with Capt. Hazzard until he met his buggy on the way to him. Upon his arrival on the plantation he was very much depressed by the state of things & the result of the crop. He has now somewhat recovered. The refusal of the negroes to ditch disturbed him very much, even more he says than the failure of the crop, as it diminished hope for the future …

Frank continued to write to Rebecca during her stay in Charleston, and his early letters of 1868 celebrate the birth of their first child, William Pringle Frost, who came into the world on December 30, 1867.

In 1869, Rebecca was expecting again, and on February 18, while still at Camp Main with Frank, she wrote to her mother expressing concerns about her husband, who was ill and taking medicines. The plantation work was demanding and dangerous; she wanted Frank to give it up, and did not wish to raise her children in the country. Later, as her second pregnancy progressed, she moved to Charleston as usual, and on April 29, 1869, Frank wrote to her from North Santee:

My very precious wife,

How can anyone who does not live in my heart know how precious, how very precious you are to me? I think of you & love you over & over again every moment of every day, and you do but seem more dear & more precious to me each time. How can I help longing for the idol of my heart, the dearest treasure, the chiefest good, the only object of my affections & desires on earth? To love you is now the fixed habit, the abiding impulse, the motive spring of my life. You are my darling wife, the bright sunshine of my inner life; my only refuge, my only solace & happiness in this world. How I do yearn for you! … Oh! Dearest, this is a bitter life without you

… And then I am always so anxious about you. Tell me, how are yr dear feet, are they still painful? How I do wish I could kiss them & sooth away all [heat] and pain! And those headaches, do they still disturb you? Do tell me, Dearest, all about yr dear self. And our precious baby, tell me how he looks, & what he does, & who admires him …

On April 1, 1871, while at South Island, Frank wrote to Rebecca in Charleston:

My very dear wife,

Yrs of today I have received. You are so good & precious that I love you more & more every day. I [do long] until I am sick to have you back with me. This life of separation wears & tears on me & keeps me most miserable & uncomfortable in body & mind. I am glad to hear such good acc'ts of our precious little ones; & yr fancied likeness of the little girl to my sainted father touches me deeply. I am here to direct some repairs to our house & to put the premises and grounds in order against yr coming. I have a heavy heart about my business, my hindrances & discouragements are so great. I see no good prospect for the future, & am very fearful of failure at both places. Mama has written me a touching letter of sympathy & counsel, wh[ich] I value very much & try to appropriate the spirit, but I feel like the troubled sea. I am troubled about my religious state & about everything on earth & can get no quiet of mind, & my only stay & comfort is absent from me all the time, my only dear, precious wife. I do like to tell you of my sufferings, & I seldom do, for I do not wish that you sh'd be burdened with my miseries …

The following week, Rebecca penned a reply:

Dearest,

I went to Church & took the Communion. I felt so full of gratitude to the Gracious God, Who had so filled me with blessings & mercies. I don't think I ever enjoyed the services so much. I thought how we had stood together before that Altar, & made our marriage vows before God, how we had communed together, & how we had brought our little ones there to be signed with the sign of the Cross, & how we hope to bring another. I yearn so to have you at my side, & was with you in prayerful as well as loving thoughts. Your dear Mother's sweet face brightened with tenderness & pleasure as her eyes caught mine, as I looked toward her on entering the church. I loved her so for your dear sake, as well as for all her gentle virtues. No heart but yours could know all the mercies I had to thank God for, and only God could read the [unuttered], unexpressed prayers for my precious ones that stirred my heart. I could but say as I left God's house, 'Lord now lettest Thou Thy servant depart in peace.' I hope you had a pleasant day, dear Love, & that you did not miss me too much. I will be ready to go back, whenever you come … With truest love, I am your devoted Wife.

On June 8, 1869, another son, Edward, was born to Rebecca and Frank, and about two years later, on March 14, 1871, Rebecca gave birth to their first daughter, Mary.

Pringle family letters of May and June 1871 are full of sad news about the last illness and death of Rebecca's younger brother James Reid Pringle. He had been living in California, where he married Coralie Butterworth in 1868. Their first child, Henry, was born in 1869. In early May 1871, the Pringle family in Charleston received an urgent telegram notifying them that James was "hopelessly ill." A month later, he lay dying at the Breevort Hotel in New York. His wife Cora (who was expecting their second child) and her family were with James, and Rebecca's parents, her brother William, and her sisters

Susan and Mary traveled to New York to be with their loved one during his last hours.

James Reid Pringle died on June 9, 1871, and a few days later, Susan Pringle wrote to her sister Rebecca about the family's loss:

You have heard the sad story dearest Sister, that dearest James is dead. Oh my God! how hard it is to realize, altho' we watched the last hours of our beloved … We found Mary weeping in the hotel, to welcome us, & then they took us in to see our beloved. We found him very feeble, but he recognized us. He was too ill to be dressed & sitting up that day, but I am sure none of the Drs [doctors] understood his case. Brother sat up with him that night, & he was very restless, delirious indeed. But in the morning Thursday, when Mama & I went down before six, he knew us all, said, 'It is so sweet to have you all around me in peace & love & harmony, my Father, my Mother, so sweet, so sweet. You will not leave me again. You will stay by me, until I close my eyes forever, until God calls me away.' Oh Rebecca it is impossible to describe the touching accents in which he spoke. Then he stretched out his arm, & said, 'Mother put your head here, & come close to me, dear Mother, so sweet to have you here. You will not leave me again. Cora all this time, could not believe in his danger. She clung to his life in any way, but we knew he was dying. All day Thursday he was so low & feeble we thought he could not live many hours. Mama & Papa sat up with him that night. When I went down early Friday morning he knew me again & put up his dear lips to kiss me … his voice was very faint, & I had to put my ear down to hear what he was trying to say. It was 'Our Father, say Our Father' & oh you should have seen the peace that came over his dear face as I knelt down & prayed … Then I brought his boy, his beautiful smiling boy to him, & he kissed him, & kissed us all again, & called for Cora. It was the most touching thing to see that beautiful child with his dying father … Well we watched him all day, dying, & he did not speak again but thank God there was no convulsion, no struggle. He just breathed away his life, & died precisely at 12 Friday night. It was a blessed beautiful death, but with all the consolation we have had, so terribly sad. He had so much to live for, a lovely, devoted wife, & this most beautiful boy, for he is really one of the handsomest children I have ever seen, fair prospects in life, & loved & respected by all and so good. Oh Rebecca it is wonderful to hear how good he was … Cora's grief is very touching … they would not let her stay with him a great deal on acct of her condition … She clung to me all the time, & said, 'Sue tell me what <u>am</u> I to do. I cannot live without him. Oh if God would only let me die with him.'

About four months later, another family tragedy was to strike. In late September, little Edward Frost fell ill, and Rebecca took him Charleston for medical care. On October 18, she wrote to tell her husband Frank that Edward's condition had worsened:

Dearest,

You will be sadly disappointed – our precious little Edward lies in the most critical condition. God only knows how the scales will turn. The fever that I wrote you had suddenly set in on Saturday morning, abated only to return on Monday, since when it has not left him, & with it has appeared that distressing inability to retain nourishment … I have but little hope that our precious child will be spared. I try to assign all to our heavenly Father, but, oh the pain of watching the sufferings of our gentle, & once so bright little one …

Edward Frost, who was less than two and a half years old, died the next day. His grieving mother wrote to her sister Susan Pringle:

... The loss of our bright little one is an ever freshening sorrow – so sad that while nearly all others have escaped, our brave little one is gone. The child was so full of promise. I cannot help deploring him – he never gave me trouble – only joy and filled me with pride ... How can I help regretting the absence of what was so beautiful and brave – Pringle says 'Mother, God took Edward to Heaven because he was such a good boy.' I feel the chastening is meant for me so worldly and presumptuous I am. I think all will have to be taken before I can have more faith. It is well God's compassion faileth not. His mercies must be new every morning else we would be destroyed again and again...

In the first month of 1873, Rebecca was again in Charleston with her family awaiting the imminent birth of another child. On January 7, she wrote to her husband, who was at South Island:

My beloved Husband,

I have been longing for your presence so intensely, that you would come in the steamer yesterday. I was grateful for your letter, poor substitute as it was. I have been loving you more than ever, since you left me, if indeed that <u>were</u> possible. Dearest, you will <u>never</u> know in this world, how true & unceasing my love for you is, and how often I thank God for the blessing of such a good man. When I find fault with you it is only because my love is all concentrated on <u>you</u>. I wish I did not make myself so miserable because you are away from me. I trust God will so bless us, that we may be spared to be with each other, without any <u>further</u> or <u>future</u> separation. I do not like to think of your being at South Island. It must be so cold for you ...

A daughter, Susan Pringle Frost, was born on January 31, 1873. Towards the end of that year, on December 5, Rebecca wrote to Frank:

My beloved Husband,

It is such a gloomy day that I am thinking of you with more than usual anxiety, for I know how dull you are today, fretting so about your work. I wish I were with you, we would have such a nice day together, never mind I am going to be back with you soon, & then I mean to keep house so nicely for you, & fix up everything so nicely … If you knew how I long to feel your dear arms around me, you would never doubt that your love <u>alone</u> is all I need for happiness. I am only telling you of these wishes to tease you dearest. I am so happy in your love. When I think of you, that you are my own dear Husband, I do feel so happy, I don't care for anything else. I can't feel so uneasy about the future as you do, for the thought of the wealth I possess in you makes me feel I would be throwing away such a blessing. No, no, as long as your dear life & love are preserved to me, I will not be over anxious …

Over the next two years, Rebecca would bear two more children who were named for their parents – a son, Francis, born March 26, 1875, and a daughter, Rebecca Motte Frost, who was born on August 12, 1877.

In 1876, Frank finally gave up the life of a planter. One of his last letters to Rebecca from Camp Main, written on May 8, 1876, is a sweet tribute to her:

My dearest wife,

I am so full of love & tenderness for you tonight that, altho' I have just finished my letter, I will continue my communings with my darling one, the idol of my heart ... I have been longing so for you tonight, that I have taken out all of yr sweet letters to me written before our marriage, & have read them with so much pleasure & gratitude, & have felt so entirely unworthy of the pure, virgin love & the simple, guileless confidence wh[ich] you expressed. I have loved you, darling, with my whole heart, passionately, & I have been entirely true to you, but it has been all due to yr own beautiful self. You have commanded & constrained my love & admiration ... You are so pure & guileless & truthful & confiding, so devoted & tender a wife, so beautiful & dutiful a mother ...

The end of a planter's life on the North Santee River, however, did not mean the end of separations for Mr. and Mrs. Frost. A letter of January 21, 1878, identifies Dr. Francis L. Frost as a traveling agent for the Stono Phosphate Company, and husband and wife were often parted because of his business trips. In early February 1879, he wrote to Rebecca from Montgomery, Alabama:

My dearest wife,

I am missing you exceedingly today. It does seem so very hard that I sh'd be so constantly separated from the one object which is most dear & congenial to me on earth. Life is passing so rapidly, & the only sweetness that there is in it to me (my dearest wife) is lost to me. How I do yearn for the companionship of my dearest one, my only one in fact ... You are too beautiful & lovely, Darling, & I cannot tell you what delight I find in you, even in thinking of you. Your dear features & figure are constantly looming up before me, even in my dreams, & I am filled with inexpressible tenderness for you.

I trust that you are well, Darling. You are so hard worked & look so thin, & I am so little able to take that tender care of you which is necessary that I am all the time full of the most painful anxieties about you ... I have been to church today, & have walked all over the city, but the uppermost & almost the only thought has been of my darling wife.

Toward the end of 1879, on December 2, Frank was in Augusta, Georgia, and lamented to his wife:

My dearest wife,

Business has detained me here a day longer. I trust that you continue well in mind & body. I am full of love for you, & you are ever most tenderly in my thoughts. You are my own precious, loving & beautiful wife, & I love you with all the ardor & romance of our early attachment ...

The next day, Rebecca answered from Charleston:

My own beloved Husband

... Thanks for your sweet, sweet letter, which came last evening. Be sure that I shall heed every word of it. Dear, dear Husband, how good you are, how pure & noble. No one can know but myself. Thank God for such a blessing. How sweet to feel I can place entire confidence in you. To think that you are my own true Husband. What a blessing to know that I shall never fear an unkind word from your lips. For myself I can claim only true love to you, darling, a love which grows deeper & deeper every year. The anniversary of our happy wedding day is near at hand. How richly God has blessed us! Do not let us throw away our happiness by fretting over small trials. Make the best of our blessings while we still have them. Do not think of me as being otherwise than happy. I am happier than anyone around me. How could I be otherwise with such a Husband.

The love letters between Frank and Rebecca continued into the 1880s, and their devotion to each other never dimmed, as shown in this excerpt from a letter of April 3, 1881, which Frank wrote from Macon, Georgia:

> My dear, sweet wife
> … I am so glad to hear from my Darling & to know that she & the dear children are well … I long for you Dearest, for yr sweet dear companionship at all times, but especially on Sunday, & more than I can express … Love to Mary & Susan, & the dear children & very sweet wife, whom I love with frantic devotion …

Their love was indeed, as their daughter Susan noted, "deep-seated and eternal." Rebecca passed away in 1905, and Frank survived her until 1912. They are both buried at Magnolia Cemetery in Charleston.

BIBLIOGRAPHY

Chesnut, Mary Boykin. *A Diary from Dixie.* New York: D. Appleton & Company, 1905.

Cote, Richard N. *Mary's World: Love, War, and Family Ties in Nineteenth Century Charleston.* Mount Pleasant, S.C.: Corinthian Books, 2001.

Daly, Louise Porter Haskell. *Alexander Cheves Haskell: Portrait of a Man.* Wilmington, N.C.: Broadfoot Publishing Company, 1989.

De Leon, Thomas Cooper. *Belles, Beaux and Brains of the 60's.* New York: G. W. Dillingham Company, 1909.

DuBose, William Porcher. *The Reason of Life.* New York: Longman, Green & Company, 1911.

DuBose, William Porcher. *Turning Points in My Life.* New York: Longmans, Green & Company, 1912.

Dunham, Chester F. *The Attitude of the Northern Clergy Toward the South, 1860-1865.* Philadelphia, Pa.: Porcupine Press, 1974.

Frost, Mary Pringle. *The Miles Brewton House: Chronicles and Reminiscences.* Charleston, S.C.: Privately printed, 1939.

Johnson, John Lipscomb. *The University Memorial: Biographical Sketches of Alumni of the University of Virginia Who Fell in the Confederate War*. Baltimore: Turnbull Brothers, 1871.

Manigault, Gabriel. "The Lowcountry of South Carolina" *The Land We Love* 2 (November 1866).

Perry, Hext McCall. *Letters of My Father to My Mother, Beginning with Those Written During Their Engagement*. Philadelphia, Pa.: Avil Printing Company, 1889.

Wallace, David Duncan. *The History of South Carolina*. New York: The American Historical Society, 1935. Volume 3.

Manuscripts & Archival Sources

Alston-Pringle-Frost Papers. South Carolina Historical Society (SCHS)

DuBose, William Porcher. "Reminiscences." Southern Historical Collection, University of North Carolina.

Frost, Susan Pringle. "Jottings." In the Alston-Pringle-Frost Papers at SCHS.

Louis Manigault Family Record. SCHS

Porter Family Papers. SCHS

Queen Victoria's Journals, Royal Archives. RA VIC/MAIN/Q VJ (W) 10 February 1840 (Princess Beatrice's copies)

William Porcher DuBose Correspondence. SCHS

ABOUT THE AUTHOR

KAREN STOKES has worked with historical manuscripts at the South Carolina Historical Society for over twenty years, and her special area of interest is the Confederate period in the Palmetto State. She is the author of numerous articles and books, and her recent non-fiction works include *South Carolina Civilians in Sherman's Path, The Immortal 600,* and *Confederate South Carolina.* She has also co-edited and published collections of the wartime letters of two Confederate officers, *Faith, Valor and Devotion* and *A Confederate Englishman,* and has authored four works of historical fiction including *Honor in the Dust* and *The Immortals.*

ALSO BY KAREN STOKES

AVAILABLE FROM SHOTWELL PUBLISHING

SOUTHERN STUDIES

A Legion of Devils: Sherman in South Carolina by Karen Stokes

Annals of the Stupid Party: Republicans Before Trump by Clyde N. Wilson (The Wilson Files 2)

Confederaphobia: An American Epidemic by Paul C. Graham

Dismantling the Republic by Jerry C. Brewer

Dixie Rising: Rules for Rebels by James R. Kennedy

Emancipation Hell: The Tragedy Wrought by Lincoln's Emancipation Proclamation by Kirkpatrick Sale

Lies My Teacher Told Me: The True History of the War for Southern Independence by Clyde N. Wilson

Maryland, My Maryland: The Cultural Cleansing of a Small Southern State by Joyce Bennett.

Nullification: Reclaiming Consent of the Governed by Clyde N. Wilson (The Wilson Files 2)

Punished with Poverty: The Suffering South by James R. & Walter D. Kennedy

Segregation: Federal Policy or Racism? by John Chodes.

Southern Independence. Why War? — The War to Prevent by Dr. Charles T. Pace

Southerner, Take Your Stand! by John Vinson

Washington's KKK: The Union League During Southern Reconstruction by John Chodes.

When the Yankees Come: Former South Carolina Slaves Remember Sherman's Invasion. Edited with Introduction by Paul C. Graham

The Yankee Problem: An American Dilemma by Clyde N. Wilson (The Wilson Files 1)

FICTION

GREEN ALTAR BOOKS
LITERARY IMPRINT

A New England Romance & Other SOUTHERN Stories by Randall Ivey

Tiller (Clay Bank County, IV) by James Everett Kibler

GOLD-BUG MYSTERIES
MYSTERY & THRILLER IMPRINT

To Jekyll and Hide by Martin L. Wilson

PUBLISHER'S NOTE

IF YOU ENJOYED THIS BOOK or found it useful, interesting, or informative, we'd be very grateful if you would post a brief review of it on the retailer's website.

In the current political and cultural climate, it is important that we get accurate, Southern-friendly material into the hands of our friends and neighbours. *Your support can really make a difference* in helping us unapologetically celebrate and defend our Southern heritage, culture, history, and home!

For more information, or to sign-up for notification
of forthcoming titles, please visit us at

WWW.SHOTWELLPUBLISHING.COM

SOUTHERN WITHOUT APOLOGY

Made in the USA
Columbia, SC
20 February 2018